JOHNNY JOHNNY HAS GOOD HAIR!

ANGELA Y. NIXON

JENIS GROUP, LLC

Johnny Johnny Has Good Hair Copyright © 2018

Any unauthorized reproduction, use, copying, distribution or sale of these materials – including words and illustrations – without written consent of the author is strictly prohibited. Federal law provides severe penalties for unauthorized reproduction, use, copying or distribution of copyrighted material.

For bulk order prices or any other queries, please contact aynixon@angelaynixon.com

Book Cover design by Angela Y. Nixon
ISBN: 978-1-942674-24-5

First Edition: April 2018

This book belongs to

_____

Johnny Johnny
has good hair.
Only touch it if you dare!

Using a comb
with extra care,
Johnny Johnny makes
styles with lots of flair!

He wears his hair flat
when he's in a hurry,

It's quick to do, so
then he can scurry!

He wears his hair high when he wants to feel tall.

He has to be careful though, or his hair could fall!

He wears his hair fluffy when he's feeling cool.

It was a popular style when he was in school!

Johnny Johnny is also a dapper boy!

He wears suits and ties with so much joy!

His ties are purple,
green, and blue.

Now Johnny Johnny
will show them
all to you!

His purple tie makes
him feel happy.

His blue tie makes
him feel extra sappy.

And his green tie is for times whenever...

Johnny Johnny wants to feel really clever!

One day Johnny Johnny came home rather sad.

Some people made him feel really bad.

They said his hair and ties were weird.

They laughed and joked and stared and sneered.

"Go home!" They said. "And change your silly hair!"

"Take off that tie as well while you're there!"

Johhny Johnny walked home and cried.

The people shouted, "Put on something simplified!"

"We're sorry we had to make a fuss,"

"But you should try to dress more like us!"

Johnny Johnny didn't know what to do.

Should he change his hair and stop wearing ties too?

But Johnny Johnny loved his hair and the way he dressed.

Why should he fit in with the rest?

With a new brave
feeling on the way,
Johnny puffed out his
chest to say,

I am who I am
and that's okay!
I'll wear funky hair
and ties anyway!

I am who I am and that's okay!

I'll wear funky hair and ties anyway!

Now Johnny Johnny proudly does his hair,

And he wears his fun ties everywhere!

www.ingramcontent.com/pod-product-compliance
Lightning Source LLC
Chambersburg PA
CBHW051351110526
44591CB00025B/2967